THE FORMER SOVIET STATES

BELARUS, UKRAINE, AND MOLDOVA

By
Kelvin Gosnell

The Millbrook Press
Brookfield, Connecticut

Reprinted in 1993

©Aladdin Books Ltd 1992
Designed and produced by
Aladdin Books Ltd
28 Percy Street
London W1P 9FF

First published in the
United States in 1992 by
The Millbrook Press
2 Old New Milford Road
Brookfield, Connecticut 06804

The consultant is Dr. John Channon of the School of
Slavonic and Eastern European Studies, London, U.K.

Series Design: David West
Designer: Rob Hillier
Editor: Claire Watts
Picture Research: Emma Krikler

Library of Congress Cataloging-in-Publication Data

Gosnell, Kelvin.
    Belarus, Ukraine, and Moldova/by Kelvin Gosnell:
John Channon, consultant.
       p. cm -- (Former Soviet States)
    Includes bibliographical references and index.
    Summary: Compares and contrasts the three former
Soviet republics of Belarus, Ukraine, and Moldova, linked
by geography and economics
    ISBN 1-56294-306-5 (lib bdg.)
    1. Soviet Union, Northwestern--Juvenile literature. 2.
Belarus--Juvenile literature. 3. Ukraine--Juvenile literature.
4. Moldova--Juvenile literature. (1. Belarus. 2. Ukraine.
3. Moldova.)
I. Title. II. Series.
DK501.8..G67 1992
947--dc20   92-2241 CIP AC

CONTENTS

INTRODUCTION

Belarus, Ukraine, and Moldova lie along the western border of the former Union of Soviet Socialist Republics (U.S.S.R.). Together they stretch from the Baltic states in the north to the Black Sea in the south. Throughout the centuries, great foreign armies have rolled across these vast flat lands, Vikings and Mongols, Nazis and Russians, bringing slaughter and misery to the local people.

There are no mountains or other natural boundaries to separate different areas within Belarus, Ukraine, and Moldova. Instead, people have used language and religion to maintain their national identities. The only obstacles are the great, wide rivers such as the Dnepr and the Dnestr. From the earliest times, traders have used the network of great rivers for transportation, coming from as far afield as China and Scandinavia, settling on the riverbanks, and building great cities which have somehow withstood the trials of multiple changes of ownership.

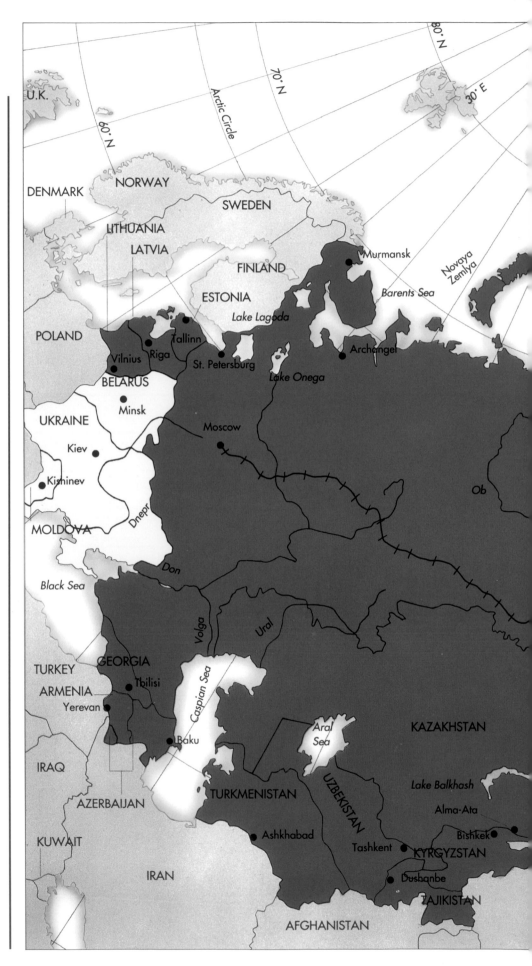

4

Arctic Ocean

Zemlya Frantsa Josifa

Severnaya Zemlya

Novo Sibirskiye Ostrova

Laptev Sea

Kara Sea

70° E

80° E

90° E

120° E

130° E

140° E

150° E

160° E

170° E

Kolyma

Bering Sea

Lena

Yenisey

Sea of Okhotsk

50° N

Sakhalin

RUSSIAN FEDERATION

JAPAN

Trans-Siberian Railroad

Lake Baikal

Vladivostok

40° N

NORTH KOREA

SOUTH KOREA

MONGOLIA

CHINA

0	250	500	750	1000	1250 MILES
0	500	1000	1500	2000 KILOMETERS

THE STATES TODAY

In Minsk, the capital of Belarus, the leaders of the founding member states of the Commonwealth of Independent States (C.I.S.) met in December 1991 to sign the historic accord which put an end to the Soviet Union. The Soviet Union collapsed because communism, its political ideology, was discredited; claiming to deliver economic benefits, it had, on the contrary, reduced many of its 300 million citizens to poverty.

An attempt to reform the Soviet system by the last president of the Soviet Union, Mikhail Gorbachev, was beginning to show some signs of success when a group of Gorbachev's closest advisers launched a coup in August 1991, attempting to bring back many of the worst aspects of the Soviet regime, including press censorship, restoration of the powers of the secret police, and suppression of political debate. The failure of this coup led ultimately to the breakup of the Soviet Union.

Independence

In Moldova, in September 1990, Mircea Snegur was elected president, and in 1991, Moldova declared its independence from the Soviet Union. In 1990, the Ukrainian parliament adopted a declaration that all its laws took precedence over those of the Soviet Union. In December 1991, Ukrainians overwhelmingly voted for independence and elected a new president, former communist party leader Leonid Kravchuk. Belarus also declared its independence in 1991.

Of the fifteen former member republics of the Soviet Union, the three founder-signatories at that initial meeting on December 9 in Minsk were the republics of Russia, Belarus, and Ukraine. Later, they were joined by a total of eight more, including Moldova. The C.I.S. was

Leonid Kravchuk votes in Ukraine's independence referendum.

Independence rally, Kiev

intended to coordinate members' foreign policy, set up a single economic zone, draw up a customs and immigration policy, and develop transportation and communications. Existing borders were to be recognized and the aims of the United Nations (U.N.) respected. Belarus, Ukraine, and Moldova already had their own seats at the U.N., a concession which had been won by Stalin at the time when the U.N. was set up following World War II.

Establishing an identity

The C.I.S. was set up to help deal with some of the problems created by the breakup of the Soviet Union, but, while member states look to one another for support, they are anxious to establish their own identities.

Ukraine has decided to return to its medieval unit of currency, the grivna. Moldova announced its intentions to switch from the Russian ruble to the lei, as in Romania. Belarus adopted it's own currency also called the ruble.

The Crimean crisis

In 1954, Nikita Khrushchev, leader of the Soviet Union, gave the Crimea to Ukraine. The majority of the region's population is Russian, and they feel that Khrushchev's transfer was illegal. Ukraine is anxious to hold onto the Crimea, a beautiful area with an important tourist industry. The problem is further confused by the return to the area of Crimean Tatars, deported by Stalin to central Asia after World War II. The Tatars would prefer independence for their ancestral lands.

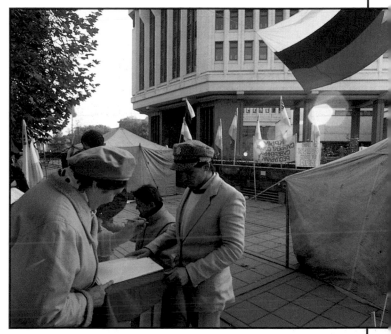

Republican activists in the Crimea

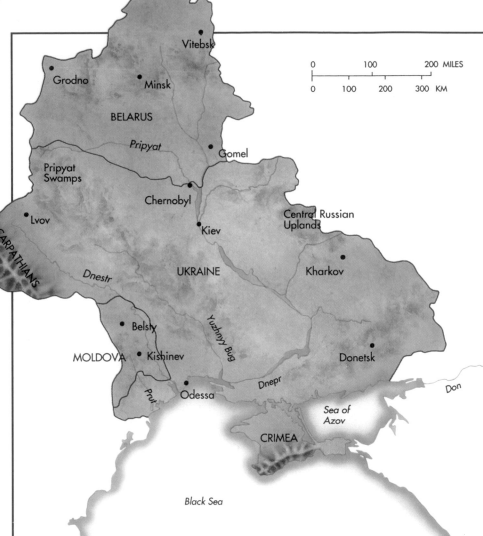

Ukrainian prairie farming

PEOPLE AND PLACES

The Belovezh forest in Belarus is the largest ancient forest left in Europe, where rare European bison roam between 500-year-old oaks and giant pines. Forests cover one third of the country and are vital to Belarussian industries such as paper and furniture making. The swampland that covers 10 percent of south and west Belarus is very fertile when drained, so there is much land reclamation. There is also coal and oil beneath the Pripyat Swamps in the south.

The black earth

Ukraine's economic importance is second only to Russia's in the former Soviet Union. Ukraine boasts rich coal fields, iron ore mines, and important industries such as space technology. To the north of the country is forest; farther south stretches the famous Russian steppe, less wooded and more grassy. South of Kiev stretches an ocean of flat prairie, the rich, fertile "black earth" land of the Ukraine. At the beginning of the century, Ukraine exported a huge amount of grain, earning the name "the breadbasket of Europe" and, more recently, the state produced 20 percent of the total agricultural output of the Soviet Union.

Second smallest state

Moldova, the second smallest state of the former Soviet Union, lies in the arc of the Carpathian Mountains, surrounded on three sides by Ukraine and on the fourth by Romania. The Moldovian people are ethnic Romanians, and they have struggled for centuries to be united with their Romanian neighbors. Like Ukraine, Moldova's black soil is rich and fertile.

The religious divide

Most of the people of Belarus, Ukraine, and Moldova are Christian, although they are divided among three different churches. Some belong to the Roman Catholic Church, and acknowledge the Pope as the head of the church. Others belong to the Eastern Orthodox Church, which was originally based in the Byzantine capital of Constantinople. These two churches were split in 1054 over questions of beliefs and customs.

Several attempts to heal the rift were made but in 1596 several million Orthodox Christians formed the Uniate Church, which acknowledges the authority of the Pope in Rome, but retains the liturgy, language, customs, and dress of the Orthodox Church.

Chernobyl

At 1:23 a.m. on April 26, 1986, the Number 4 reactor at the Chernobyl nuclear power station in Ukraine exploded. A massive cloud of radioactive dust was released into the atmosphere, contaminating a vast area of northwestern Europe. It is now calculated that up to 100,000 people, especially in the immediate vicinity, will die prematurely from radioactivity-related diseases as a result of the accident.

Many populated areas were evacuated after the Chernobyl disaster.

EARLIEST TIMES

The zone of mixed forests and swamplands known as Belarus, or White Russia, was the homeland of Slavic peoples as long ago as 2000 B.C. Hunters, fishermen, and beekeepers, they traded their furs, game, fish, honey, and wax along the network of rivers running between the Baltic and the Black seas. Early Slav settlements were based on the islands of dry ground in forest clearings and along the rivers where traders met and bartered their goods.

The Scythians were originally a nomadic tribe. In the seventh century

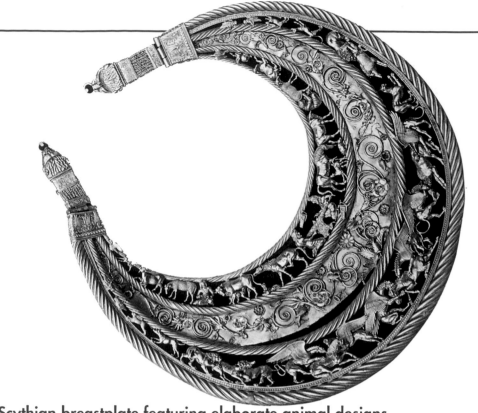

Scythian breastplate featuring elaborate animal designs

Scythian death mask

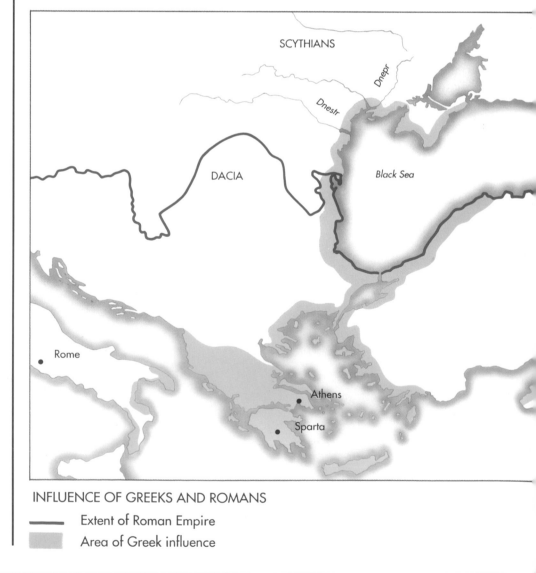

INFLUENCE OF GREEKS AND ROMANS

⎯⎯ Extent of Roman Empire

▨ Area of Greek influence

B.C., they settled in the steppe lands adjoining the Black Sea from the Carpathian Mountains to the banks of the Don River. They traded wheat for luxury goods in nearby Greek colonies.

Dacia

There were Greek trading colonies around Moldova in the seventh century B.C., when the region was known as Dacia. The Dacians were influenced by the Scythians, but had their own rulers until Dacia became a province of Rome, following the invasion in A.D.105 by the Roman emperor Trajan. The Romans ruled Dacia for 163 years until waves of invaders from the east overwhelmed them. The Romans left behind the ruins of various fortifications and sufficient remnants of their legions to give a name and character to the Romanian language.

The Khazars ruled the southern steppe in the eighth century A.D. They were a group of tribes of many nationalities and religions, horsemen and traders who expanded from their original base in the northern Caucasus. By the tenth century they had been completely eclipsed by the coming of a new power: the Rus.

Viking hordes

The Vikings, or Varangians as they were known in Russia, were fierce Scandinavian warriors whose longboats became a signal for terror all around the coast of Europe and the Mediterranean. They established a trading base at Novgorod. In A.D. 878, they seized the settlement of Kiev as a base from which to launch raids. The name "Rus" which was given to the Viking kingdom in Kiev may be derived from the Finnish word "routsi" for rowers.

Viking invaders raid the coast of Europe.

KIEVAN RUS

Between A.D. 800 and 1240, Kievan Rus became one of the world's great centers of trade and power. Rus was a loosely organized group of city-states run by robber-baron princes. They were probably descendants of the Varangian invaders, as often at war with each other as with the neighboring Magyars and Khazars around the Dnestr and Dnepr where they flow into the Black Sea. The capital of Rus, Kiev, became a major city and grew rich on

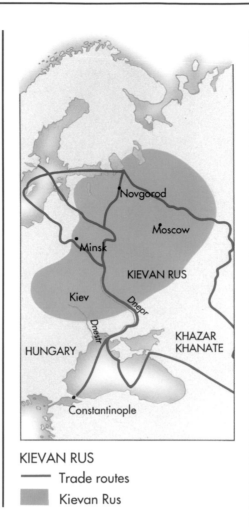

KIEVAN RUS
— Trade routes
▨ Kievan Rus

The Church of Hagia Sophia, Constantinople

trade in amber, furs, and slaves from the north in exchange for the silks and spices of Constantinople.

The Byzantine or eastern Roman Empire was enormously wealthy, because it was the hub of east-west trade. Banking and commerce were highly developed there. Raiders from Kiev arrived annually in the Byzantine capital, Constantinople, to carry on a mixture of trade and threatening demands for tribute, formalized as early as 907 as a treaty.

Sviatoslav I united the territory of Kievan Rus with the Azov peninsula. He defeated the Khazars in battle and headed off to conquer Bulgaria. He was stopped by a Byzantine army, retreated, and then was ambushed and killed on his way back to Kiev in 972. A period of bloody struggles began between Sviatoslav's sons, ending in 977 with the triumph of Vladimir.

The coming of Christianity

While his father had extended the territory of Rus, Vladimir made it stable, establishing a legal and political structure. In 988, having researched the major alternative religions, Islam, Judaism, Roman Christianity, and Orthodox Christianity, Vladimir converted to Orthodox Christianity. His messengers had reported that the Orthodox rite they had witnessed at the basilica of Hagia Sophia in Constantinople was so beautiful, "We knew not whether we were in Heaven or on Earth." The conversion of Rus to Christianity is one of the most important landmarks in the history of the Russian people.

Decline
The decline of Kiev began with the decline of east-west trade routes. The crusades reestablished traditional routes via the Mediterranean and Adriatic seas by making Muslim lands safe for

The crown of the Russian tsars

Cossacks are famed for their horse-backriding.

The Cossacks
Along the southern border of Rus lived the Cossacks, wild bands of wandering bandits, making a living by hunting, thieving, and living off the land. By the time the Mongols came, the Cossacks were Orthodox Christians, usually at the service of the Russian tsars. Occasionally though, the Cossacks allied themselves with the Khans of the Golden Horde, the descendants of Mongols who had settled around the Don delta and were known as the Crimean Tatars.

Christian travelers. This meant that the route via the Baltic and the Black seas was less convenient and less profitable. Kiev lost control of the Azov peninsula in the late eleventh century.

But worse was to come. In 1223, a Mongol army defeated the Russians. The Mongols were a savage horde of warriors from the east led by Genghis Khan who swept across Europe, looting and murdering. Fourteen years later, the Mongols came back with a vengeance, sacking every Russian town that resisted and imposing their rule for the next two hundred years.

THE RISE OF POLAND

By the time the Mongols from the east had destroyed the fragile union of Rus, Poland and Lithuania already dominated a vast area of central Europe, from which they moved farther east and south into Belarus, Ukraine, and Moldova. Poland was Catholic and Lithuania was heathen in 1386, when they were united by the marriage of Prince Jagiello of Lithuania and 14-year-old Jadwiga, heiress to the throne of Poland. Jagiello converted to Roman Catholicism as a condition of the match. The two countries, although united, continued to be administered separately.

"The Ukraina"
In 1569, Lithuania ceded the southern half of its lands to Poland in return for guarantees of assistance against the rising might of Muscovy, the Orthodox Russian state which had succeeded Kievan Rus. These lands became known as the "Ukraina," or frontier, and were henceforth subject to increased Polish influence.

Polish landlords had huge estates in Ukraine, where they treated their Ukrainian peasants as if they were Polish serfs. The towns were increasingly populated by Jewish traders and artisans and other German-speaking incomers, administered by a special law adapted from that of Magdeburg in Germany. There was pressure on Orthodox believers to convert to

A Polish gentleman

Roman Catholicism, or at least to the Uniate Church. Under this pressure, an intellectual resistance movement sprang up in the Monastery of the Caves in Kiev, where monks promoted Orthodox theology through sermons and other literary works.

The four hundred years during which Belarus and Ukraine were under Polish-Lithuanian rule created considerable differences between them and the developing state of Muscovy. These conflicts have become the subject of much debate over the last hundred years and are at the heart of present-day negotiations about the future relationship between all three republics.

Cossack risings
In 1648, the Ukrainian Cossacks led by Bohdan Khmelnytsky rose against their Polish overlords. By 1654, it had become clear that independence could only be won with armed assistance either from the Turks or from the tsar in Moscow. Khmelnytsky persuaded his fellow Cossacks to seek the protection of the

GROWTH OF POLAND AND LITHUANIA

- ⬜ Lithuania to 1300
- ⬜ Lithuania to 1341
- ⬜ Lithuania to 1377
- ⬛ Lithuania to 1386
- — Boundary after 1386

Meanwhile, in Belarus, the Poles yielded territory to their powerful eastern neighbor, Moscow. Tsar Alexis took Smolensk, and Catherine the Great (1729-96) took more territory in 1772 and 1792. By 1794, the whole of present-day Belarus was part of the Russian Empire. Finally, in 1812, Moldova was ceded to Russia by the Treaty of Bucharest. Thus, Ukraine, Moldova, and Belarus all became part of the Russian empire and increasingly subject to Russification. The use of the Ukrainian and Belarussian languages was banned during the nineteenth century.

tsar. Khmelnytsky died in 1657, and after a period of fighting it became clear to the Cossacks that Moscow's intentions were to assimilate Ukraine rather than be its ally.

Russification

In consequence of its strategic position, giving access to the Danube and the Balkans, Moldova always had to play off its most powerful neighbors against each other. In the sixteenth and seventeenth centuries these were the Poles and the mighty Ottoman Empire.

In 1652, a daughter of Vasily Lupu, ruler of Bessarabia, part of Moldova, had married Khmelnytsky. After Ukraine was united with Russia in 1654, an embassy from Moldova went to seek protection from Tsar Alexis (1645-76) against the Turks. But it took another 150 years before Moscow took control of Moldova.

Catherine the Great

Attack on the life of Alexander II, 1881

TSARIST RULE

The nineteenth century Russian state ran the largest system of forced labor on earth. Nobody except the tsar was free. At the bottom were serfs, divided into private and state-owned. Serfs had to live and work where official records said they belonged. Landlords and merchants also had to yield the state services or money, and needed permission to travel abroad. As in the modern Soviet state which succeeded it, the vast majority of state expenditure was military. Methods of collecting taxes led to widespread corruption.

Decembrist uprising
Two secret reforming societies sprang up, founded after the Napoleonic wars by former army officers who were discontented with the country's government. Pavel Pestel was the leader of the Kiev group. His plans for change were startlingly similar to the outcome of the coup of 1917 which eventually toppled the tsar. He proposed to shoot the royal family and merge "weak races" into one Russian-dominated state. Among the "weak races" he included Belarussians, Ukrainians, and Bessarabians.

The Decembrist uprising of Pestel's group and the St. Petersburg branch took place in 1825 during the confusion caused by the succession of Grand Duke Nicholas, after the unexpected death of Tsar Alexander I. The revolt failed and its leaders were executed or sent to Siberia.

Napoleon at the Battle of Smolensk, 1812

Poland had come under Russian administration after the defeat of Napoleon in 1815. In 1830, a nationalist uprising was defeated and Tsar Nicholas I took strong measures to discourage any future uprisings in the empire. There was great pressure on the Uniate Church to return to Orthodoxy. In Ukraine, the Magdeburg Law was revoked, removing certain civil rights from town-dwellers. Thousands of people were deported to Siberia, and many villages in Ukraine, accused of sympathizing with the Poles, were burned by Russian troops.

The Crimean War
In 1853, Russian troops moved into Moldova, which they had temporarily evacuated under the terms of an international agreement to demilitarize the Black Sea in 1841. France, Britain, and Turkey objected, and sent troops to the Crimea. After an inglorious campaign, during which most casualties on both sides were caused by the unsanitary conditions, peace terms were agreed upon, under which Russia ceded part of Bessarabia acquired in 1812 and renounced any special role in Moldova.

Revolution from above
Tsar Alexander II came to the throne in 1855, aware that social and economic reforms had to be made: "Better revolution from above than from below," he said. In 1861, the serfs were finally emancipated in a way which effectively passed power from the nobility to the Russian bureaucracy. The peasants had exchanged one form of servitude for another. There was bitter disappointment. For a time, however, the economy did take off. Then, in 1905, Russia was shaken by revolution. A spectacularly unsuccessful war with Japan had brought a great many human casualties and economic ruin, which paralyzed the government. Throughout the empire, there were nationalist murmurings, strikes, and calls for "land for the people." A series of government-inspired pogroms against the Jews drove many into the growing revolutionary movements. At long last, a program of thorough reform was undertaken by Russia's first elected body, the Duma. But before this had time to develop, Russia was plunged into World War I.

The defense of Sebastopol during the Crimean War

REVOLUTION

In 1917, the suffering caused by World War I and the political unrest in the country led to riots in Petrograd. The tsar, Nicholas II, was forced to abdicate and a provisional government took over. Many exiles began to return to the country, including Vladimir Ilyich Lenin, who had left after the failure of the 1905 revolution. By October, it was clear that the provisional government was failing to address people's problems or put an end to the war. The Bolsheviks, led by Lenin, seized power.

Civil war broke out and the former Russian Empire was in turmoil.

Independence hopes

The coup seemed to offer Ukraine a renewed opportunity for independence. Ukrainian nationalism had survived tsarist rule as a largely underground movement based in Lvov. A central council met in Kiev in 1917 and declared that an independent Ukrainian republic had come into being. In February 1918, at the end of the war, the Central powers signed a separate peace treaty with the republic. Almost immediately, the Bolshevik Red Army intervened and established a communist government in Kiev. Western Ukrainians, armed and supported by the Poles and Austrians and led by Simon Petlyura, resisted until March 1921, when Belarus was divided between Poland and the future Soviet Union.

The socialist governments of Belarus, Ukraine, Russia, and Transcaucasia agreed to form a federation. It was agreed that national languages should take precedence within each republic, and many émigrés returned. A New Economic Policy (N.E.P.) was introduced which allowed a certain amount of individual enterprise.

Stalin

All this came to an abrupt end, however, when Joseph Stalin took over as leader of the Soviet

Joseph Stalin

The Red Army crosses the Dnepr, 1920.

Union. Under Lenin, Leon Trotsky had been the Soviet Union's second-in-command. After Lenin's death in 1924, however, a bitter power struggle began, and Stalin emerged triumphant. In 1928, Stalin reintroduced Russian as the official language of the Ukraine and abandoned the N.E.P. Political show trials and persecution of intellectuals and other leaders followed, accompanied by mass executions and deportations to prison colonies known as gulags, in a reign of terror that was to last nearly a quarter of a century.

Carol I of Romania

United Romania

In the mid-nineteenth century, demands were made in Moldova and its sister principality Walachia, for the unification of all Romanians in one kingdom. Unification was achieved in 1859, but Bessarabia was ceded to Russia less than twenty years later in the Treaty of Berlin, which settled the last Russo-Turkish war in 1878. In 1881, the kingdom of Romania was set up under King Carol I, a magnet for Moldovan nationalism.

SOVIET EXPANSION

Throughout the 1920s, Romania worked to establish a series of European alliances to discourage the Soviet Union from pressing claims to Bessarabia. One of its allies was Poland, which was also in dispute with the Soviet Union over Belarussian and Ukrainian territory. A world economic crisis in the 1930s created political difficulties for the Romanian government, threatened by the rise of totalitarian parties.

Fascism, a political creed which encouraged racism and violence, gained power in Italy and Germany under Mussolini and Hitler. A fascist group called the Iron Guard sprang up in Moldova. In an attempt to prevent the fascists from taking power, King Carol II of Romania proclaimed a dictatorship in 1937. The Iron Guard continued to stir up unrest with German encouragement, and all hopes of resistance faded when it became known that Germany and the Soviet Union had signed a pact in August 1939.

World War II

Germany invaded Poland in September 1939, upon which Britain declared war. France fell to the Germans in 1940, and in June the Soviet Union occupied Bessarabia and northern Bukovina. Soon after, Romania was forced to cede territory and 3.5 million subjects to the Soviet Union, 2.4 million to Hungary, and 360,000 to Bulgaria. Under German

Adolf Hitler

leadership, Romanian forces crossed the Dnestr into Soviet territory in 1942, where they organized the Romanian province of Transnistria. After the battle of Stalingrad in 1944, the tide turned against Germany. A coup overthrew the Romanian

The Battle for Kiev, 1943

government in 1944 and restored Carol II's son, Michael, to the throne. But by now Soviet troops occupied Romania and they set about installing a communist government. In 1947, Michael was forced to abdicate and Bessarabia was ceded to the Soviet Union.

Belarus suffered appalling losses during World War II. One in four of the population died as the Germans and then the Soviet armies occupied the territory. Three quarters of all housing and almost all industrial buildings were destroyed. In 1945, the peace treaty between the Soviet Union and Poland left most of western Belarus in Soviet hands.

After World War II, Moldova, Belarus, and Ukraine underwent profound change. Before the war, the majority of the population lived and worked in the country. By 1979, more than half lived in cities. Russians moved in large numbers to occupy positions of power in industry and government. Stalin ordered the removal of whole peoples, including the Crimean Tatars, from

Former Moldovian national emblem

their homelands as punishment for fighting alongside the Germans during the war. They have waged a campaign to return ever since.

Ukrainian hopes

During the 1930s, a Ukrainian nationalist movement continued to exist in Poland. When Germany started World War II, Ukrainian nationalists hoped for German support to create an independent state and some joined the Axis forces. However, the Nazi government of Germany envisaged taking over the rich lands of Ukraine, and behaved with barbarous cruelty toward the people. The combined forces of the Soviet Union, the United States, Britain, and France defeated Nazi Germany and victory brought gains of territory to the Ukrainian Soviet Socialist Republic.

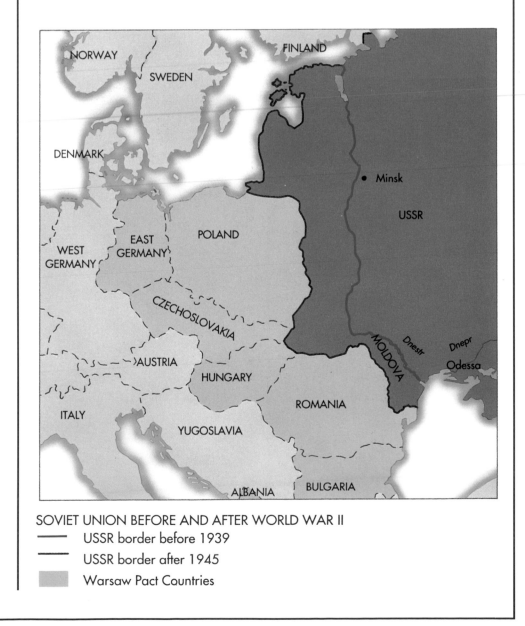

SOVIET UNION BEFORE AND AFTER WORLD WAR II

—— USSR border before 1939

—— USSR border after 1945

Warsaw Pact Countries

Lithuanians at an independence rally celebrate the collapse of communist Romainia.

SINCE GORBACHEV

By 1985, it was clear in all three republics that the communist social, economic, and political system based in Moscow was in deep trouble. The new leader of the Soviet Union, Mikhail Gorbachev, announced a program of *glasnost,* or openness, and *perestroika,* or re-building. Each republic had its own agenda for change and different organizations pressing for it. In Ukraine, Rukh, the popular movement for *perestroika*, demanded that the truth be told about matters such as the mass murders under Stalin and the Soviet government-induced famine of 1932-33, when millions died in Ukraine. After Chernobyl, there were also demands for an end to nuclear-power generation and permission to organize a popular front along the lines of those in the Baltic States.

The collapse of communism

Meanwhile, just outside the borders of the Soviet Union in Eastern Europe, revolution was in the air. The communist leader of Romania, Nicolae Ceausescu was toppled in a coup in December 1989, precipitating changes over which neither Bucharest nor Moscow had any control. Within the Soviet Union, fighting broke out in Transnistria between Russian and Ukrainian speakers, aided and sanctioned by Cossack mercenaries and Romanian speakers. The old guard clung to power in Ukraine, where communist party chief Shcherbitsky held on until November 1989, when he was replaced by Vladimir Ivashko.

All over Eastern Europe, people were rising up against Soviet-run socialist governments and discovering that this time there would be no armed opposition from the Red Army. Amid scenes of rejoicing, in December 1989 the Berlin Wall, symbol of the division of Europe for over thirty years, was opened.

The Soviet Union's economic crisis led to long queues even for basic foods.

In Ukraine, elections were held in March 1990 in which Rukh, in alliance with other parties opposed to the communist government, gained one quarter of the seats. There were increased demands for the return of many Uniate Churches which had been appropriated by the Russian Orthodox Church.

An attempted coup

In August 1991, hardline communists closely associated with President Gorbachev attempted to reimpose the authoritarian rule of the past. Gorbachev and his family were placed under house arrest at their palatial vacation home by the Black Sea.

Russians took to the streets to defend their new parliament, led by Boris Yeltsin. The poorly organized plotters were arrested. In the aftermath, the Soviet republics made plain their desire for an end to the Soviet Union and the communist system.

Mikhail Gorbachev

National languages

In the 1960s, campaigns began for the restoration of the Ukrainian language in schools, newspapers, and public life. The Belarussian language, which is very similar to Russian, is a minority language which nationalists hope to revive. In Moldova, official recognition that "Moldovan" was in fact Romanian was finally achieved in 1989, when the Latin alphabet replaced Cyrillic. The Cyrillic alphabet was invented in the ninth century, and is used for Slavic languages such as Belarussian, Russian and Ukrainian.

STANDING ALONE

In the wake of the breakup of the Soviet Union, Belarus, Moldova, and Ukraine have the opportunity to be independent countries for the first time for centuries. However, formerly they relied on the support of the mighty Soviet Union to give them economic and military backup. Today they need the support of other countries to help them stand as states in their own right.

The economy
As with the whole of the former Soviet Union, the economy of the region is a vital issue needing urgent attention. The problems Gorbachev started to address have yet to be solved and massive amounts of foreign investment are needed. One of the major ironies of the collapse of the Soviet Union is the boast that it was a "worker's paradise." Elementary commodities, such as soap, are hard to come by. Many country roads are mud tracks, impassable in spring. Farming enterprise is struggling to revive after decades of direction from the government, deprived of contact with market forces. There is widespread corruption, evident everywhere, but particularly marked in Moldova and western Ukraine, a major smuggling route for contraband to and from the West. Half the rural hospitals and clinics have no sewage connection, many have no hot water system, and some have no piped water at all. There are shortages of all medical supplies from bandages and anesthetics to disposable needles.

The disputed Soviet Navy in the Crimean port of Sebastopol

The C.I.S. summit, December 1991

As the extent of the economic collapse became known, many Western European charities such as the Red Cross launched appeals to provide food and medicine to the people. A Bank for East European Reconstruction and Development was started to provide capital for industry. The United States and the International Monetary Fund (I.M.F.) promised to provide funds to stabilize local currencies in return for action by governments to clarify land ownership and other laws of property.

Neighbors

The future of the C.I.S. is uncertain, as the new states argue among themselves over weapons, borders, and valuable natural resources. In the field of weaponry, Russia and Ukraine dispute the future of the warships of the former Soviet Navy, based in the Ukrainian port of Sebastopol. Also, Ukraine delayed implementing an agreement to send all its nuclear arms to Russia. It is possible that the C.I.S. may end up as an economic union, like the European Community.

Moldova may look to satisfy its ethnic Romanian population by unification with its neighbor, Romania. This would not suit the many Russians, Ukrainians, and other peoples who have settled in the state.

The Crimean question concerns not only Ukraine and Russia but also the Turkish government, which has expressed an interest in the plight of the Muslim Crimean Tatars. If their rights are not taken into consideration, Turkey might consider economic or even military pressure.

The Lenin hydroelectric station on the Dnepr

OUTLOOK

At home, all three states face similar problems. After generations of foreign rule, they must establish a strong political and economic system as soon as possible.

Minorities

Ukraine and Moldova face major problems with national minorities within their borders, and questions regarding the borders themselves. There was a great deal of population movement during the period of Soviet rule. The borderlands of the Dnestr River between Moldova and Ukraine have been fought over many times. It is one of the areas traditionally patrolled on behalf of the rulers of Russia by Cossack soldiers, who continue in this role today. A long-standing policy of resettlement of Russians and Ukrainians in Moldovian cities has complicated the issue further.

A border dispute dating back centuries reopened over Transnistria on the northeast shore of the Dnestr River, between Ukrainians and Russians resident in the area and native Moldovians. Cossack mercenaries have weighed in on the side of Ukrainians and Russians who want the territory to be part of Ukraine. Russian-speaking residents of Transnistria know that Moldova is likely to rejoin Romania.

Environmental damage

Pollution of air, soil, and water is a major problem. The Don and Dnepr are open sewers, polluted by untreated industrial waste. Soil erosion has damaged the lands in the south. In Ukraine and Belarus, there is the fatal legacy of Chernobyl, the world's worst nuclear accident. Thousands of acres of fertile agricultural land and hundreds of villages have been rendered unusable and uninhabitable.

Looking to the future

Belarus, Ukraine, and Moldova all have abundant natural resources and well-developed industries, from the rich lumber resources of Belarus to Ukraine's world-famous space technology industry. Even without the Crimea, Ukraine's beautiful Black Sea coast is a great tourist attraction. Black Sea ports, such as Odessa, are a vital trade route from the states of the former Soviet Union, since northern ports are closed for up to five months of the year due to weather conditions.

With the support of their neighbors and the rest of the world, Belarus, Ukraine, and Moldova have a strong base to build their independence on.

Electron microscope works, Ukraine

Crimean solar power station

FACTS AND FIGURES

BELARUS
Area: 80,200 square miles (207,000 square kilometers)
Capital: Minsk
Population: 10.3 million
Highest point: Mt. Dzyayzhynskaya 1,135 feet (346 meters)
Rivers: Dnepr, Neman
Climate: Mild with much rain
Vegetation: Forests cover one third of the land
Wildlife: European bison, hare, boar, elk, wolf
Agriculture: Lumber, beef, potatoes, sugar beet, flax, grain
Industry: Petrochemical and engineering plants, tractor and truck manufacturing, lumber-related industries.
Ethnic mix: 80% Belarussian plus Ukrainians and Russians
Language: Belarussian
Religion: Christianity

UKRAINE
Area: 233,000 square miles (601,000 square kilometers)
Capital: Kiev
Population: 52 million
Highest point: Mt. Hoverla 6,762 feet (2,028 meters)
Rivers: Dnepr, Dnestr
Climate: Mainly temperate; Black Sea region, Mediterranean
Vegetation: Forest, steppe
Wildlife: Wolf, wildcat, wild pig, gopher
Agriculture: Wheat and other grains, corn, sugar beet, meat and dairy products, grain
Industry: Coal, gas, iron, steel, space technology, military equipment, tractors, airplane engines
Ethnic mix: 75% Ukrainian, 20% Russian
Language: Ukrainian
Religion: Christianity

MOLDOVA
Area: 13,000 square miles (32,500 square kilometers)
Capital: Kishinev
Population: 4.4 million
Highest point: Mt. Balaneskty 1,409 feet (423 meters)
Rivers: Dnestr, Prut
Climate: Warm with mild winter
Vegetation: Forest, steppe
Wildlife: Boar, deer, wolf, polecat, fox
Agriculture: Wine, grapes, grain, tobacco
Industry: Food

NATURAL VEGETATION
- Coniferous forest
- Broad-leaved forest
- Grassland
- Evergreen trees and shrubs

INDUSTRY
- Metal working/machine building
- Electricity generation
- Coal mining
- Iron ore

processing, light machine building, leather, and clothing
Ethnic mix: 65% Moldovan (Romanian), plus Russians, Ukrainians, Gagauzes, Bulgarians, Cossacks
Language: Romanian
Religion: Christianity

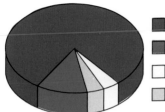

Ethnic Mix in Belarus

- 80% Belarussian
- 12% Russian
- 4% Poles
- 4% Others

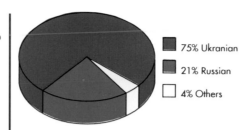

Ethnic Mix in Ukraine

- 75% Ukranian
- 21% Russian
- 4% Others

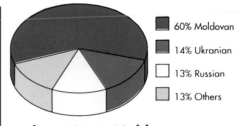

Ethnic Mix in Moldova

- 60% Moldovan
- 14% Ukranian
- 13% Russian
- 13% Others

Climate

Belarus is influenced by mild Baltic winds. Rainfall is irregular and sometimes extremely heavy. Moldova's rain comes mainly in the summer months and can cause soil erosion problems, particularly in the drier south of the country. Ukraine's climate is influenced by warm, humid air from the Atlantic Ocean. The west of the country is milder than the east during the winter and cooler in summer.

Agriculture

Ukraine was one of the former Soviet Union's most important farming states, producing one-fourth of the Union's grain. Much of the arable land of Belarus has been reclaimed from former swampland. Moldova produced one-fifth of the former Soviet Union's grape and wine output, and exported wine to some fifty countries.

Industry

Ukraine covers 2.7 percent of the former Soviet Union's territory, but accounted for 20 percent of industrial output. In Belarus, most industry uses imported raw materials, but there is a petroleum-based chemical industry and lumber-related industries. Moldova's industry is diversified, including building materials and machine-building.

Transportation

Belarus and Ukraine rely on a network of canals and rivers for transportation of raw materials and goods. The flat land of all three states has also facilitated the development of highways and railroads. Belarus is the only one of the states to have an international airport. Ukrainian Black Sea docks handled 20 percent of the Soviet Union's ocean freight.

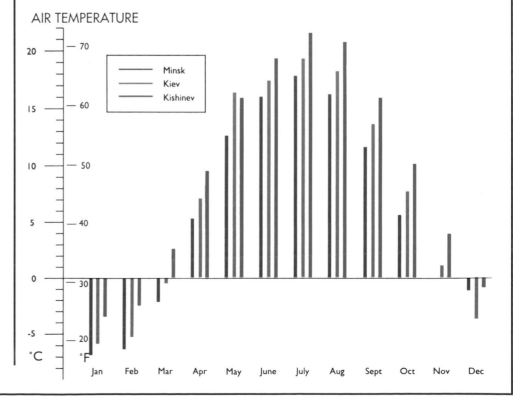

AIR TEMPERATURE

Minsk
Kiev
Kishinev

CHRONOLOGY AND FAMOUS PEOPLE

7th century B.C.
Scythians occupy Black
Sea coast
1st century A.D. Roman
invasion of Dacia
A.D.105 Trajan moves
into Dacia
8th century A.D. Khazars
occupy Black Sea Littoral
from the Volga to the
Dnestr
9th century A.D. The
state of Rus is born
977 Vladimir succeeds to
throne in Kiev
988 The state of Rus
adopts Christianity
1238-1240 Mongol
conquest of Rus
1370 Ruler of Moldova
recognizes rule of Poland
1386 Union of Poland
and Lithuania
1453 Fall of
Constantinople
1541 Moldova falls under
Turkish power
1596 Uniate Church
founded
1648 Ukrainian revolt
against Poles led by
Bohdan Khmelnytsky
1654 Khmelnytsky places
himself under protection
of Muscovy
1667 Poland and
Muscovy divide Ukraine
between them

Vladimir I (d.1015), king
of Kievan Rus, is most
famous for bringing
Christianity to the
Russians. He also
founded new cities and
built schools, churches,
and libraries. Vladimir
married Anna, sister of
the Christian Byzantine
emperor, Basil I.

1774 Russo-Turkish war
ends. Moldova restored to
Turkey
1792 Second partition of
Poland extends Russian
border into Belarus
1794 Third partition of
Poland moves Russian
border to Brest
1812 Napoleon invades
Russia through Belarus.
Bessarabia ceded to
Russia
1825 Decembrist uprising
in St. Petersburg

Leon Trotsky (1879-
1940) was born Lev
Davidovich Bronstein, in
Ukraine. He was one of
the leaders of the
Bolshevik Revolution of
1917. After Stalin became
leader of the Soviet Union,
Trotsky was exiled and
finally murdered by
Stalin's secret police.

1854-56 Crimean War.
Russia cedes part of
Bessarabia and title
claims to Moldova
1855 Death of Tsar
Nicholas I and accession
of Tsar Alexander II
1861 Emancipation of
serfs in Russian empire
1905 First Russian
Revolution
1917 October coup in
Petrograd
1918 Moldova joins
Romania

1920 Polish army marches on Kiev

1932-3 Famine in Ukraine kills millions

1939 Soviet-German pact. Gemany invades Poland, and England declares war

1940 Germany overruns France

1941 Hitler invades Soviet Union, occupies Belarus and Ukraine

1945 Potsdam conference settles European borders

1947 Bessarabia and northern Bukovina ceded to Soviet Union

1953 Death of Stalin

1954 Transfer of Crimea to Ukraine

1956 De-Stalinization speech by Khrushchev, now first secretary of Communist Party of the Soviet Union

1964 Leonid Brezhnev appointed first secretary of C.P.S.U.

1982 Yuri Andropov succeeds Brezhnev

1984 Konstantin Chernenko succeeds Andropov

1985 Mikhail Gorbachev becomes head of Soviet Union

August 1991 Coup by communist hardliners

December 1991 Mikhail Gorbachev resigns. Boris Yeltsin takes over as head of Russian government. Soviet Union dissolved. Commonwealth of Independent States initiated

Nikolai Vasilievich Gogol (1809-52) was a Ukrainian playwright and novelist who wrote in Russian. His comic and satirical works attacked petty bureaucracy and corruption. His most famous works are *The Inspector General* and *Dead Souls*.

Taras Hryhorovych Shevchenko (1814-61) was a Ukrainian poet. Born a serf, he was freed in 1838, when he was studying at St. Petersburg Academy of Art. He was exiled for his portrayal of Ukrainian history and satire of Russian oppression of Ukraine.

Olga Valentinovna Korbut (b. 1956) was a Belarussian gymnast who leaped to world fame in the 1972 Olympics in Munich. She won three gold medals and one silver and was the first person ever to do a backward somersault on the uneven parallel bars.

INDEX

PHOTOCREDITS

All the pictures in this book were supplied by Novosti RIA apart from the front cover and pages 6, 7 top, 24 & 25: Frank Spooner Pictures; 11, 12 & 13 top: Mary Evans Picture Library; 14, 19 bottom 20 bottom & 31 left: The Hulton Picture Company; 31 right: Popperfoto

PRINTED IN BELGIUM BY
proost
INTERNATIONAL BOOK PRODUCTION